Facts About the Turkey

By Lisa Strattin

© 2019 Lisa Strattin

FREE BOOK

FREE FOR ALL SUBSCRIBERS

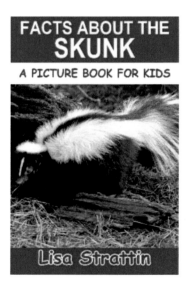

LisaStrattin.com/Subscribe-Here

BOX SET

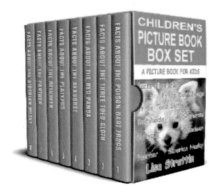

- **FACTS ABOUT THE POISON DART FROGS**
- **FACTS ABOUT THE THREE TOED SLOTH**
- **FACTS ABOUT THE RED PANDA**
- **FACTS ABOUT THE SEAHORSE**
- **FACTS ABOUT THE PLATYPUS**
- **FACTS ABOUT THE REINDEER**
- **FACTS ABOUT THE PANTHER**
- **FACTS ABOUT THE SIBERIAN HUSKY**

LisaStrattin.com/BookBundle

Facts for Kids Picture Books by Lisa Strattin

Little Blue Penguin, Vol 92

Chipmunk, Vol 5

Frilled Lizard, Vol 39

Blue and Gold Macaw, Vol 13

Poison Dart Frogs, Vol 50

Blue Tarantula, Vol 115

African Elephants, Vol 8

Amur Leopard, Vol 89

Sabre Tooth Tiger, Vol 167

Baboon, Vol 174

Sign Up for New Release Emails Here

LisaStrattin.com/subscribe-here

COVER IMAGE

https://flickr.com/photos/debarshiray/9723857258/

ADDITIONAL IMAGES

https://flickr.com/photos/dougletterman/26876592555/

https://flickr.com/photos/bigcypressnps/31635972411/

https://flickr.com/photos/dwilliss/8084133906/

https://flickr.com/photos/debiwatson/29647537504/

https://flickr.com/photos/grassrootsgroundswell/9273267091/

https://flickr.com/photos/infomastern/9305051337/

https://flickr.com/photos/debiwatson/30162437892/

https://flickr.com/photos/heypaul/2449636/

https://flickr.com/photos/amitp/14281443109/

https://flickr.com/photos/londonmatt/34711021595/

Contents

INTRODUCTION

The turkey is a large bird that is related to other game birds like pheasants, chickens and quails. The turkey has become famous across the western world as being a special meal on large family occasions including Christmas and Thanksgiving.

CHARACTERISTICS

There are two different species of turkey, the wild turkey and the ocellated turkey. The wild turkey is found naturally in the open forests of North America and weighs the most of all of the game bird species. The ocellated turkey is found in southeast Mexico and although it is the same size as the wild turkey, the ocellated turkey generally weighs half as much.

They travel in flocks and forage on the ground for nuts, berries, insects, and snails. They use their strong feet to scratch leaves and twigs out of the way, when searching for food. In early spring, the males get together in clearings to show off for females. They puff up their body feathers, flare their tails out into a fan, and strut slowly around while gobbling.

At night, turkeys fly up into trees to roost together in groups.

APPEARANCE

The wild turkey is a large, round looking bird with long, thin legs that have three toes on each foot. These help with balance and for scratching around in the dirt. The male wild turkey has a red, featherless head and throat which has small growths on it known as caruncles.

The ocellated turkey is a more elegant looking bird and, although closely related to the wild turkey, the ocellated turkey is more similar in appearance to a female peacock. The ocellated turkey has a narrow body and long legs, and the males have featherless necks and heads which can be red or blue.

Turkeys are dark overall with a bronze-green iridescence to most of their feathers. Their wings are dark, boldly barred with white. Their rump and tail feathers can be rusty or white on the tips.

LIFE STAGES

During the mating season, male turkeys make gobbling calls in order to attract a female turkey to mate. The female turkey finds a safe place to build her nest and lays between 6 to 12 eggs. These hatch after an incubation period of about a month.

LIFE SPAN

In the wild, a turkey can live for 1 to 10 years.

SIZE

Turkeys grow to be 2 to 4 feet tall and can weigh anywhere between 6 to 24 pounds.

HABITAT

Wild turkeys live in mature forests, specifically preferring nut trees such as oak, hickory, or beech, as well as edges and fields near these forests. You might see them along roads and in woodsy backyards. There are great populations of turkeys and they are not considered endangered.

DIET

The turkey is an omnivorous animal, this means that it eats both plants, bugs and small animals. The turkey prefers to eat nuts, seeds, fruits, berries and insects which it often finds while scratching around on the forest floor. However, they also eat small reptiles, amphibians and even rodents when it gets the chance.

ENEMIES

Despite its large size, both species of turkey have a number of predators within their natural environment. Foxes, snakes, raccoons, wildcats and humans are the most common predators.

SUITABILITY AS PETS

A turkey is a great choice for a pet as long as you have a good-sized yard. These are impressive looking birds with regal-looking feathers. A male turkey strutting about your yard putting its plumage on full display can be awesome to watch.

COLOR ME

COLOR ME

COLOR ME

COLOR ME

COLOR ME

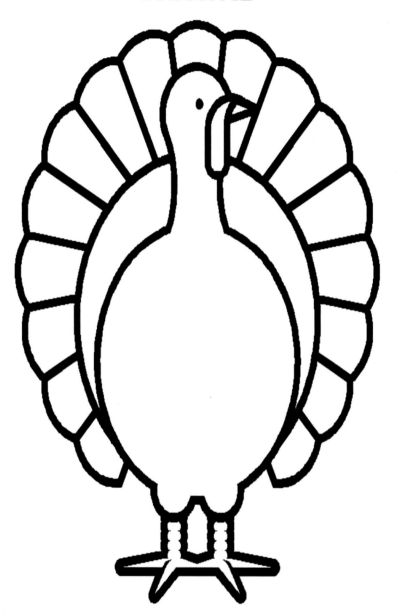

COLOR ME

COLOR ME

COLOR ME

COLOR ME

COLOR ME

Please leave me a review here:

LisaStrattin.com/Review-Vol-230

For more Kindle Downloads Visit Lisa Strattin Author Page on Amazon Author Central

amazon.com/author/lisastrattin

To see upcoming titles, visit my website at LisaStrattin.com– most books available on Kindle!

LisaStrattin.com

FREE BOOK

FOR ALL SUBSCRIBERS – SIGN UP NOW

LisaStrattin.com/Subscribe-Here

LisaStrattin.com/Facebook

LisaStrattin.com/Youtube

Made in the USA
Las Vegas, NV
21 November 2024

12309463R00026